Unit 1

Practice until students can say the words individually without help.

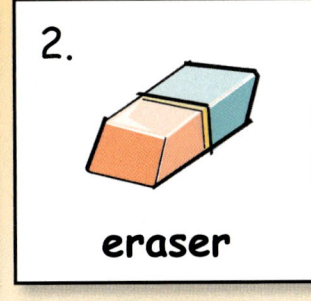

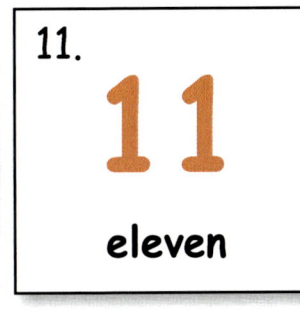

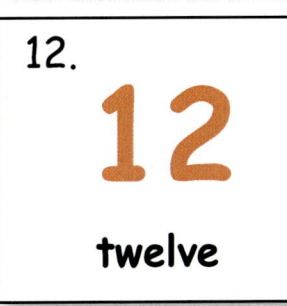

1. pencil	2. eraser	3. school bag	4. book
5. table	6. draw	7. chair	8. folder
9. door	10. game	11. eleven	12. twelve

Practice the questions together and then check in with students individually on their listening.

1. How are you?
2. What is your name?
3. How old are you?
4. Go get a pencil and eraser, please.
5. Look at me, please.
6. Sit properly, please.

Sign or Stamp

1

Students can work on this while you test them one on one on the previous page.

Read, write and draw.

1. It is a cat.

2. It is a dog.

3. It is a bed.

4. It is a kid.

1. Practice as a class. 2. Practice individually. 3. Sign or stamp only when the student can read it on their own without help.

bat

red

fun

his

hot

Sight Word:

the

Sign or Stamp

Students can work on this while you test them one on one on the previous page.

Write and find.

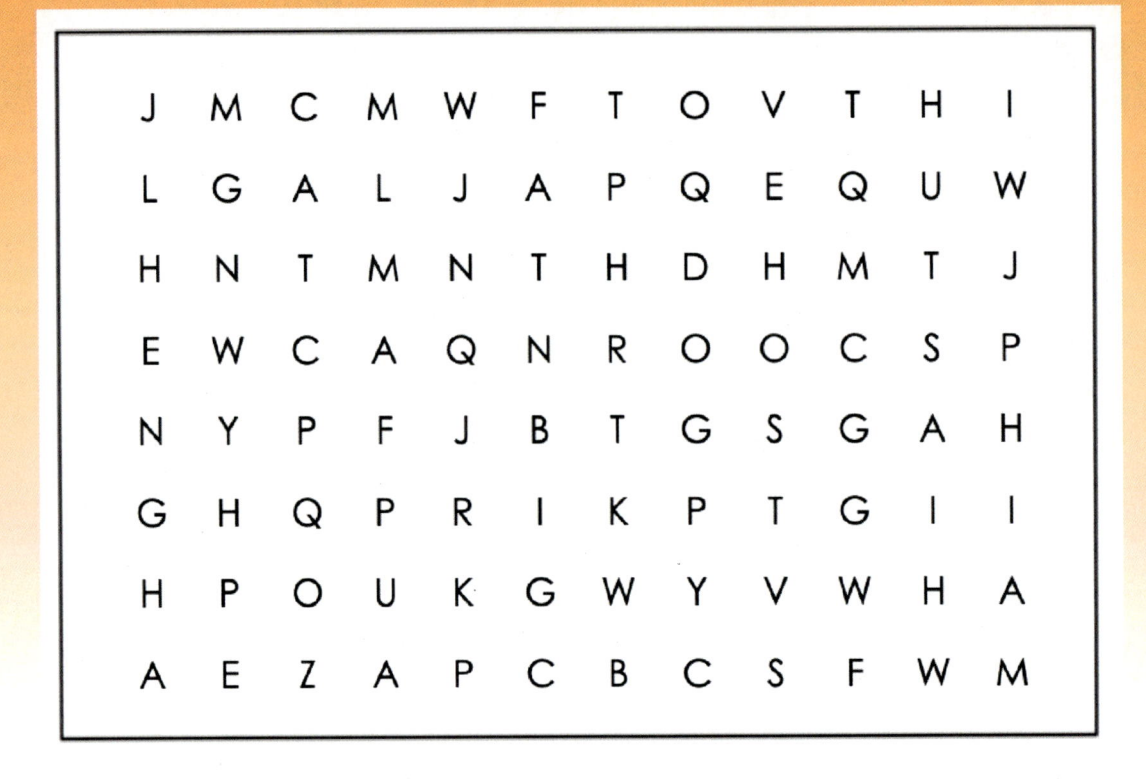

J	M	C	M	W	F	T	O	V	T	H	I
L	G	A	L	J	A	P	Q	E	Q	U	W
H	N	T	M	N	T	H	D	H	M	T	J
E	W	C	A	Q	N	R	O	O	C	S	P
N	Y	P	F	J	B	T	G	S	G	A	H
G	H	Q	P	R	I	K	P	T	G	I	I
H	P	O	U	K	G	W	Y	V	W	H	A
A	E	Z	A	P	C	B	C	S	F	W	M

BIG

FAT

CAT

HEN

DOG

HUT

4

1. Practice as a class. 2. Practice individually. 3. Sign or stamp only when the student can read it on their own without help.

The cop gets the bad pigs.
The cop puts the pigs on top.

Sign or Stamp

Students can work on this while you test them one on one on the previous page.

Unit 2

Practice until students can say the words individually without help.

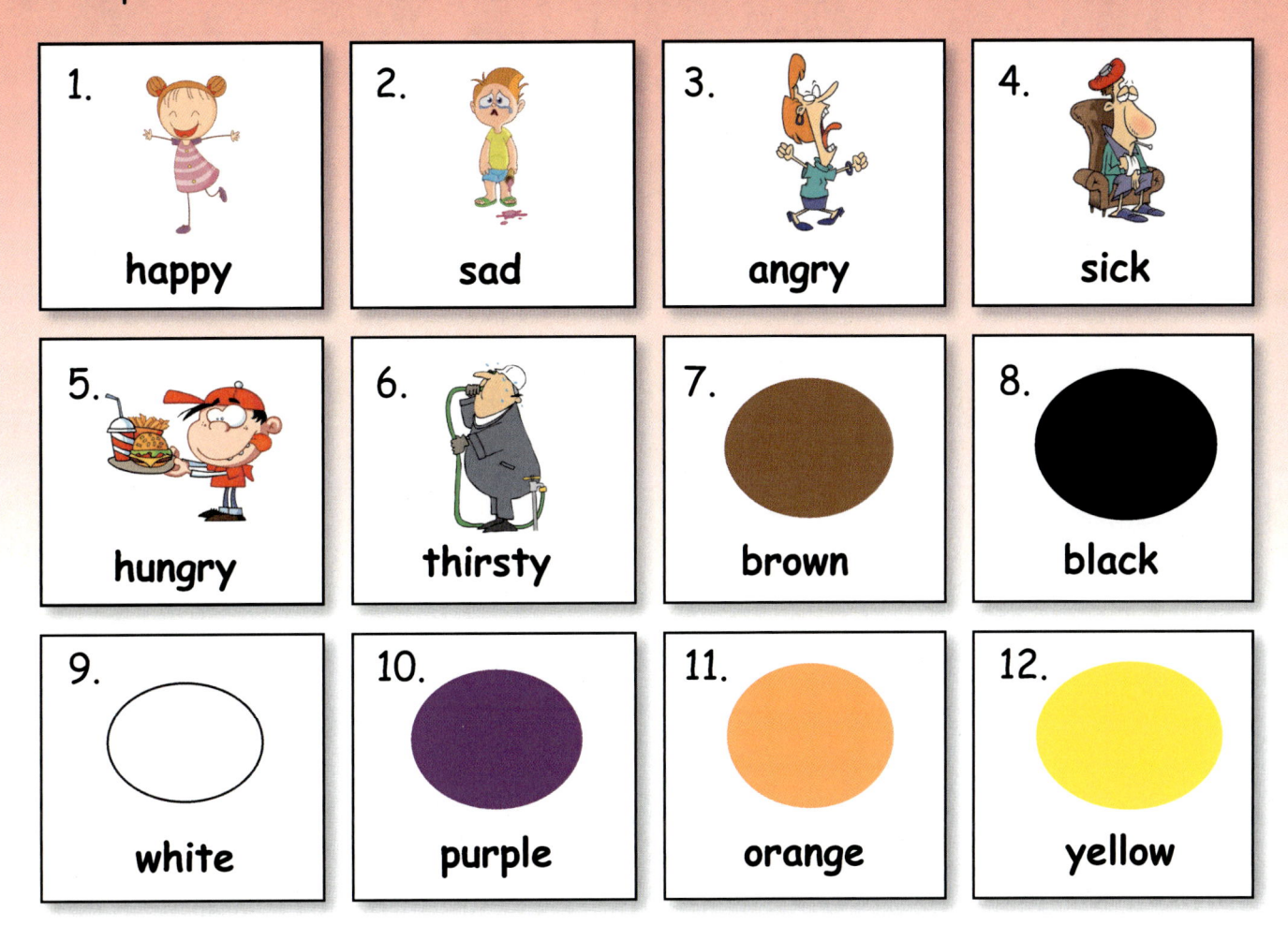

1. happy	2. sad	3. angry	4. sick
5. hungry	6. thirsty	7. brown	8. black
9. white	10. purple	11. orange	12. yellow

Practice the questions together and then check in with students individually on their listening.

1. What is your favorite color?
2. What color is this?
3. What do you like to eat?
4. Are you hungry?
5. Where is your textbook?
6. Turn to page five.

Sign or Stamp

7

Students can work on this while you test them one on one on the previous page.

Read, write and draw.

1. A cat sits.

2. A dog runs.

3. A pig runs.

4. A kid hits.

1. Practice as a class. 2. Practice individually. 3. Sign or stamp only when the student can read it on their own without help.

lad

dot

Jen

hut

pig

Sight Word:

the

Sign or Stamp

9

Students can work on this while you test them one on one on the previous page.

Write and find.

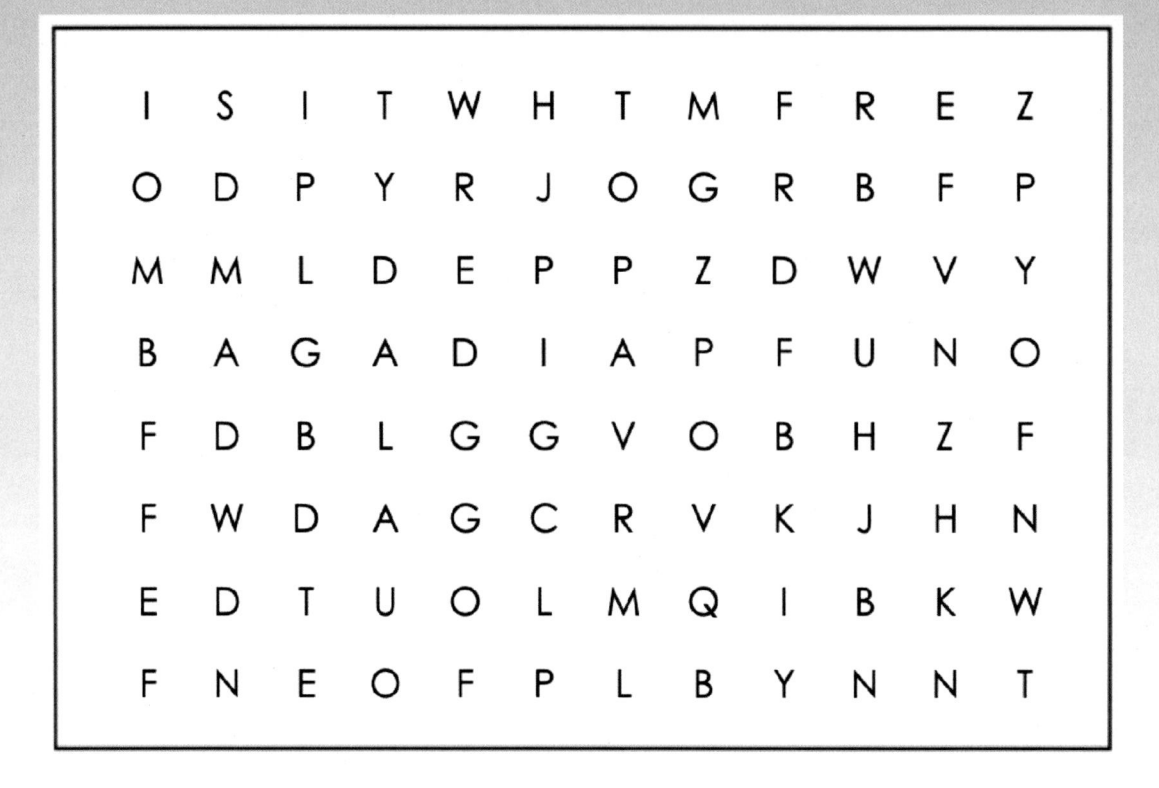

I	S	I	T	W	H	T	M	F	R	E	Z
O	D	P	Y	R	J	O	G	R	B	F	P
M	M	L	D	E	P	P	Z	D	W	V	Y
B	A	G	A	D	I	A	P	F	U	N	O
F	D	B	L	G	G	V	O	B	H	Z	F
F	W	D	A	G	C	R	V	K	J	H	N
E	D	T	U	O	L	M	Q	I	B	K	W
F	N	E	O	F	P	L	B	Y	N	N	T

FUN

RED

MAD

SIT

PIG

TOP

10

1. Practice as a class. 2. Practice individually. 3. Sign or stamp only when the student can read it on their own without help.

The dogs run. Tod wins. Jen hugs Tod. Dan is sad.

Sign or Stamp

Students can work on this while you test them one on one on the previous page.

Unit 3

Speaking Practice
Practice until students can say the words individually without help.

What can you do?
I can _____.

| 1 kick | 2 lick | 3 dance |
| 4 sing | 5 write | 6 sleep |

Listening Practice

Ask each student individually without any gestures. Sign or stamp when the student can respond correctly to all of the questions or commands.

1. What can you do?
2. Can you write your name?
3. Can you stand up?
4. Can you sit down?
5. Can you sleep?

Sign or Stamp

13

Reading Comprehension

Read, write and draw a line to the correct picture. Then color.

1. The dog licks him.

   _____
   _____
   _____

2. Jen kicks it.

   _____
   _____
   _____

14

1. Practice as a class. 2. Practice individually. 3. Sign or stamp only when the student can read it on their own without help.

ck

back

lick

duck

deck

dock

Sight Word:

go

Spelling Words:

cat

red

big

Sign or Stamp

Students can work on this while you test them one on one on the previous page.

Write and find.

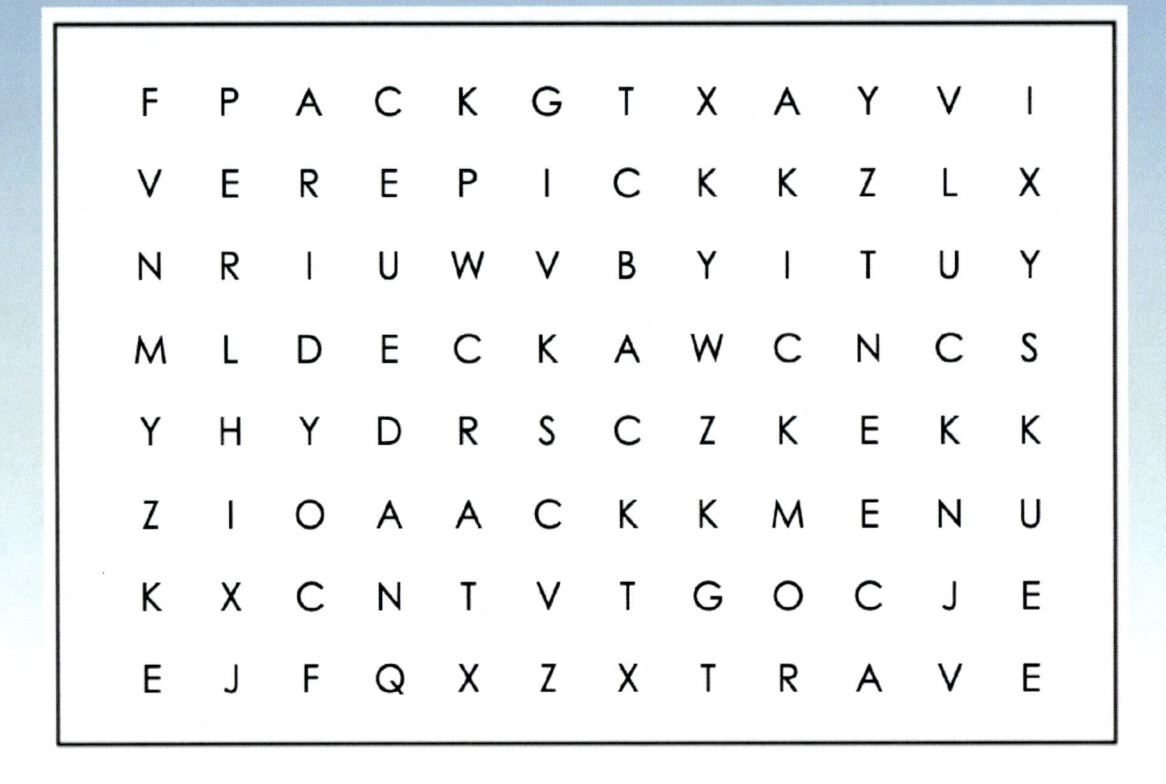

```
F  P  A  C  K  G  T  X  A  Y  V  I
V  E  R  E  P  I  C  K  K  Z  L  X
N  R  I  U  W  V  B  Y  I  T  U  Y
M  L  D  E  C  K  A  W  C  N  C  S
Y  H  Y  D  R  S  C  Z  K  E  K  K
Z  I  O  A  A  C  K  K  M  E  N  U
K  X  C  N  T  V  T  G  O  C  J  E
E  J  F  Q  X  Z  X  T  R  A  V  E
```

BACK   PICK

PACK   DECK

KICK   LUCK

1. Practice as a class. 2. Practice individually. 3. Sign or stamp only when the student can read it on their own without help.

Peg has a duck. Peg has a duck on a dock. Go, Peg!

Sign or Stamp

Students can work on this while you test them one on one on the previous page.

Unit 4

Speaking Practice
Practice until students can say the words individually without help.

Are you _____?
Yes, I am.   No, I'm not.

1 tired	2 sad	3 angry
4 hungry	5 thirsty	6 sick

Speaking Practice
Test each student individually. Act out the situations above. The student should ask you the correct question for each situation.

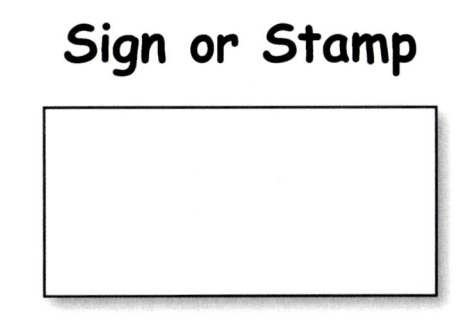

Sign or Stamp

19

Reading Comprehension

Read, write and draw a line to the correct picture. Then color.

1. The dog is sad.

2. The cat is fat.

1. Practice as a class. 2. Practice individually. 3. Sign or stamp only when the student can read it on their own without help.

st

sp

Spelling Words:
hot
fun
stop

stop

stick

past

spot

spin

gasp

Sight Word:

he

Sign or Stamp

21

Students can work on this while you test them one on one on the previous page.

Write and find.

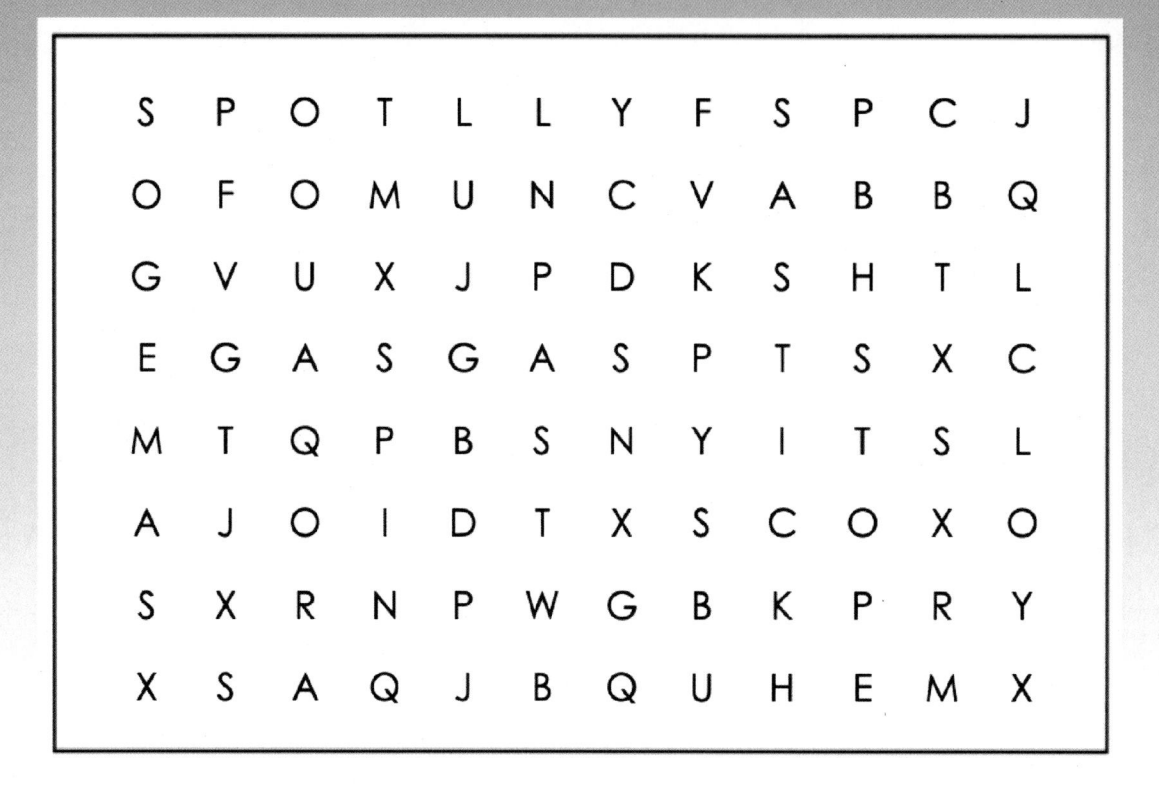

```
S P O T L L Y F S P C J
O F O M U N C V A B B Q
G V U X J P D K S H T L
E G A S G A S P T S X C
M T Q P B S N Y I T S L
A J O I D T X S C O X O
S X R N P W G B K P R Y
X S A Q J B Q U H E M X
```

STOP

GASP

PAST

SPIN

SPOT

STICK

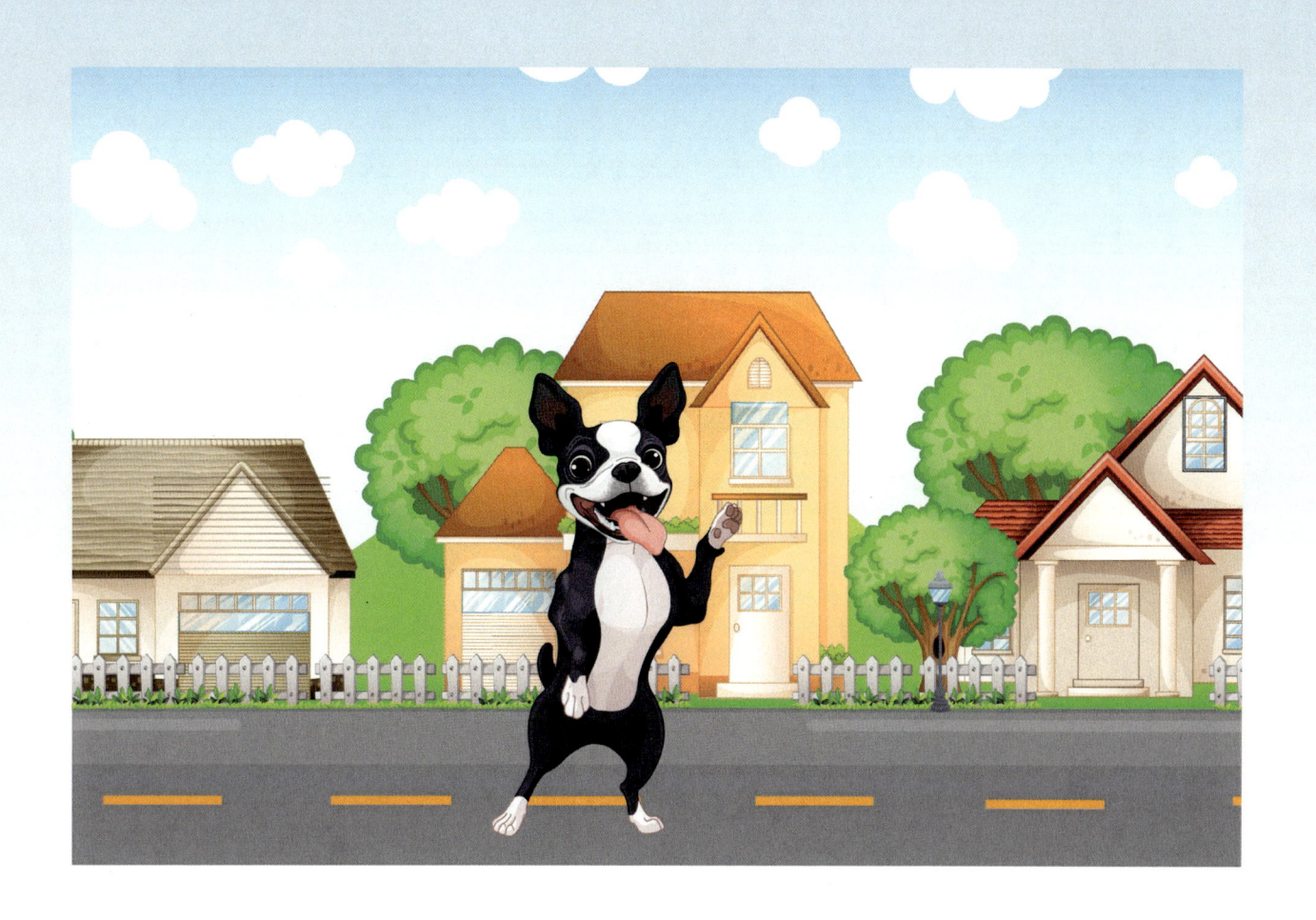

1. Practice as a class. 2. Practice individually. 3. Sign or stamp only when the student can read it on their own without help.

Spot the dog can stop. He can stand. He can spin.

Sign or Stamp

23

Students can work on this while you test them one on one on the previous page.

Review Assessments

A. Speaking

1. Practice as a class and in partners beforehand.
2. How many sentences can you make in a minute?

1. (question)   3. (question)   5. (question)   7. (question)
2. (answer)   4. (answer)   6. (answer)   8. (answer)

1. (question)   3. (question)   5. (question)   7. (question)
2. (answer)   4. (answer)   6. (answer)   8. (answer)

1. (question)   3. (question)   5. (question)   7. (question)
2. (answer)   4. (answer)   6. (answer)   8. (answer)

Review Assessments

B. Reading

How many letters and sounds can the student do in a minute without help?

It is a red dog. The red dog can run. It	11
can run fast. It gets a cat and pins it on	22
a mat. The cat is sad. Run, cat! Go, cat!	32
The cat can run fast. The dog can not	41
catch it.	43

C. Listening

Ask each student individually without gestures of any kind. How many questions out of the total does the student respond correctly to?

1. Hi, how are you?
2. What is your name?
3. How old are you?
4. What do you like to eat?
5. How many pencils do you have?
6. Are you sick?
7. Do you have a cold?
8. Do you have a cat at home?
9. What color is it?
10. Close your eyes.

D. Spelling

See how many words the students can spell correctly. The teacher says the words one by one and the students spell the words out.

cat   hot
red   fun
big   stop

Unit 5

Speaking Practice

Practice until students can say the words individually without help.

He is _____.
She is _____.

1 tall	2 short	3 cute
4 dirty	5 clean	6 smart

Listening Practice

Test each student individually. Ask the questions below without any gestures or help to see how well the student understands.

1. Where is the tall boy?
2. Where is the cute girl?
3. Who is dirty?
4. Is this girl smart?
5. Are you clean or dirty?

Sign or Stamp

Reading Comprehension

Read, write and draw a line to the correct picture. Then color.

1. The man goes.

2. The kid stops.

28

1. Practice as a class. 2. Practice individually. 3. Sign or stamp only when the student can read it on their own without help.

sk
ft

ask
desk
mask
raft
gift
soft

Sight Word:
she
are

Spelling Words:
desk
gift
are
she

Sign or Stamp

Students can work on this while you test them one on one on the previous page.

Write and find.

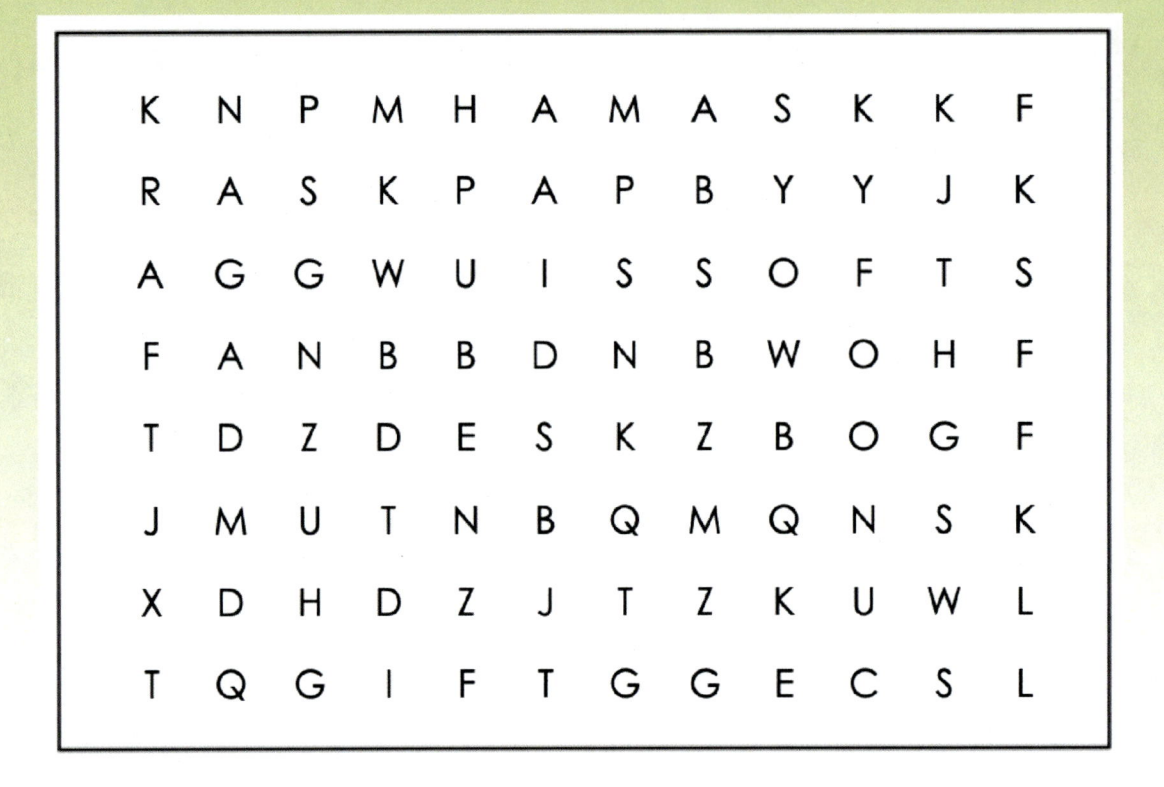

```
K N P M H A M A S K K F
R A S K P A P B Y Y J K
A G G W U I S S O F T S
F A N B B D N B W O H F
T D Z D E S K Z B O G F
J M U T N B Q M Q N S K
X D H D Z J T Z K U W L
T Q G I F T G G E C S L
```

ASK

SOFT

DESK

MASK

RAFT

GIFT

30

1. Practice as a class. 2. Practice individually. 3. Sign or stamp only when the student can read it on their own without help.

She gets a lot of gifts. The gifts are on the desk.

Sign or Stamp

Students can work on this while you test them one on one on the previous page.

Unit 6

Speaking Practice
Practice until students can say the words individually without help.

They are _____.
We are _____.

1 strong	2 fast	3 slow
4 loud	5 quiet	6 hurt

Listening Practice

Test each student individually. Ask the questions below without any gestures or help to see how well the student understands.

1. Where is the tall boy?
2. Where is the cute girl?
3. Who is dirty?
4. Is this girl smart?
5. Are you clean or dirty?
6. Are you loud or quiet?

Sign or Stamp

33

Reading Comprehension

Read, write and draw a line to the correct picture. Then color.

1. She is fast.

2. He is not fast.

1. Practice as a class. 2. Practice individually. 3. Sign or stamp only when the student can read it on their own without help.

nd
nt

and
send
hand
tent
went
bend

Sight Word:
they
want

Spelling Words:

and
went
want
they

Sign or Stamp

35

Students can work on this while you test them one on one on the previous page.

Write and find.

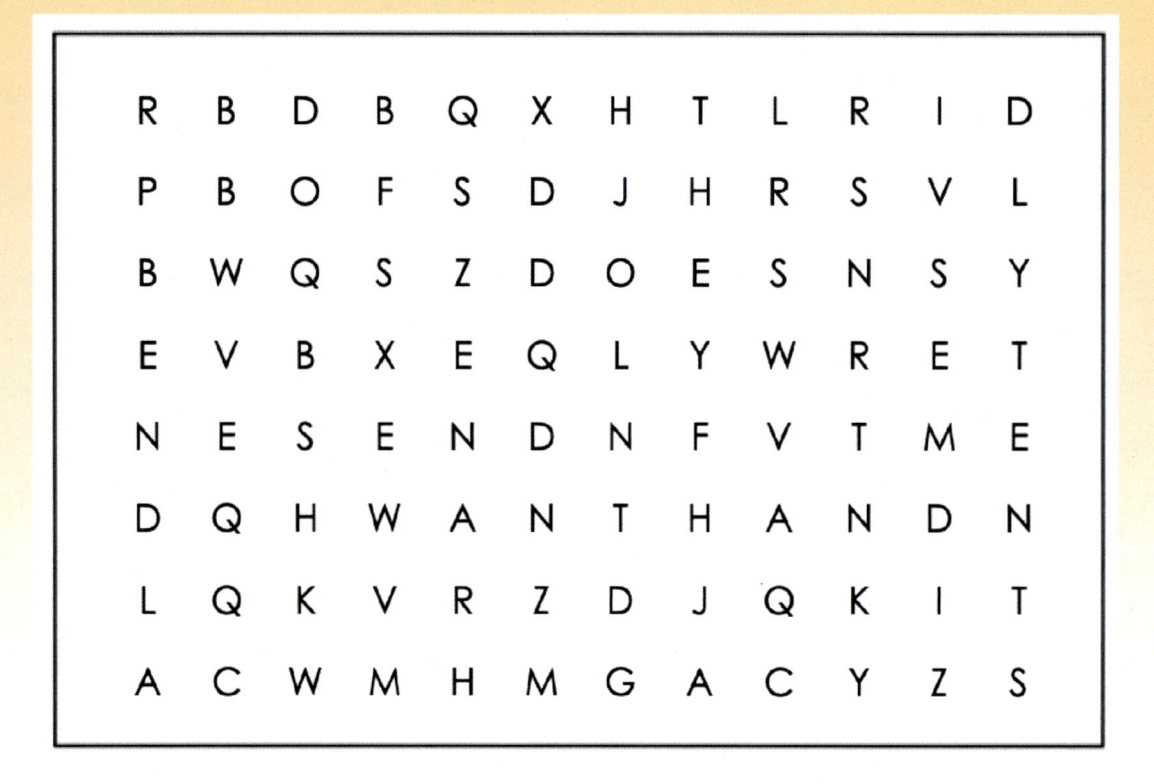

R	B	D	B	Q	X	H	T	L	R	I	D
P	B	O	F	S	D	J	H	R	S	V	L
B	W	Q	S	Z	D	O	E	S	N	S	Y
E	V	B	X	E	Q	L	Y	W	R	E	T
N	E	S	E	N	D	N	F	V	T	M	E
D	Q	H	W	A	N	T	H	A	N	D	N
L	Q	K	V	R	Z	D	J	Q	K	I	T
A	C	W	M	H	M	G	A	C	Y	Z	S

WANT
_____

HAND
_____

TENT
_____

THEY
_____

BEND
_____

SEND
_____

36

1. Practice as a class. 2. Practice individually. 3. Sign or stamp only when the student can read it on their own without help.

They want a big tent. They want to put it next to a pond.

Sign or Stamp

Students can work on this while you test them one on one on the previous page.

Unit 7

Speaking Practice
Practice until students can say the words individually without help.

What do you like to do?
I like to _____.

1 watch TV	2 swim	3 ride my bike
4 rollerblade	5 play with Legos	6 climb trees

Listening Practice

Test each student individually. Ask the questions below without any gestures or help to see how well the student understands.

1. What can you do?
2. What do you like to do?
3. Are you tall or short?
4. Are you tired?
5. Are you hungry?
6. What is your favorite color?

Sign or Stamp

Reading Comprehension

Read, write and draw a line to the correct picture. Then color.

1. The ant is on the desk.

2. The ant is on the TV.

40

1. Practice as a class. 2. Practice individually. 3. Sign or stamp only when the student can read it on their own without help.

ch
tch

chin
check
chip
catch
pitch
sketch

Sight Word:
watch
to

Spelling Words:
check
catch
the
watch

Sign or Stamp

Students can work on this while you test them one on one on the previous page.

Write and find.

C	H	I	N	Z	O	N	D	C	F	R	C
N	D	H	T	V	U	N	R	E	P	H	H
P	T	W	S	S	R	P	E	Y	C	G	I
I	W	S	K	E	T	C	H	V	H	A	P
T	M	W	Q	G	M	O	O	T	E	W	R
C	Z	G	B	E	N	N	J	W	C	R	J
H	K	S	P	C	A	T	C	H	K	P	A
L	D	P	A	E	W	G	T	K	U	C	B

CHIN

CATCH

CHECK

PITCH

CHIP

SKETCH

42

1. Practice as a class. 2. Practice individually. 3. Sign or stamp only when the student can read it on their own without help.

The witch can go fast. The witch can go fast to watch TV.

Sign or Stamp

Students can work on this while you test them one on one on the previous page.

Unit 8

Speaking Practice

Practice until students can say the words individually without help.

What do you like to eat?
I like to eat _____.

1 fruit	2 vegetables	3 hamburgers
4 French fries	5 noodles	6 rice

Listening Practice

Test each student individually. Ask the questions below without any gestures or help to see how well the student understands.

1. What can you do?
2. What do you like to do?
3. Are you tall or short?
4. Are you tired?
5. Are you hungry?
6. What is your favorite color?

Sign or Stamp

45

Reading Comprehension

Read, write and draw a line to the correct picture. Then color.

1. He can hug the dog.

2. It can catch a fish.

46

1. Practice as a class. 2. Practice individually. 3. Sign or stamp only when the student can read it on their own without help.

sh

ship
shock
cash
fish
shack
shed

Sight Word:
find
what

Spelling Words:
fish
shack
black
sand

Sign or Stamp

Students can work on this while you test them one on one on the previous page.

Write and find.

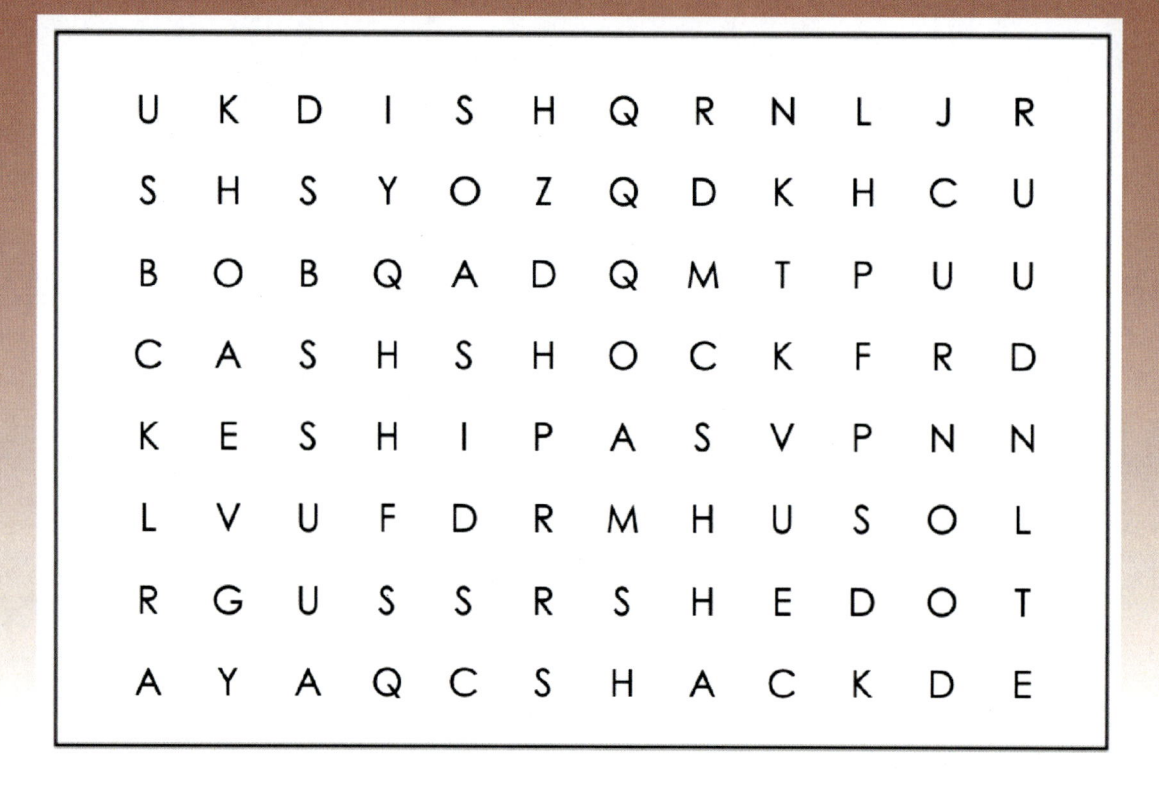

U	K	D	I	S	H	Q	R	N	L	J	R
S	H	S	Y	O	Z	Q	D	K	H	C	U
B	O	B	Q	A	D	Q	M	T	P	U	U
C	A	S	H	S	H	O	C	K	F	R	D
K	E	S	H	I	P	A	S	V	P	N	N
L	V	U	F	D	R	M	H	U	S	O	L
R	G	U	S	S	R	S	H	E	D	O	T
A	Y	A	Q	C	S	H	A	C	K	D	E

SHIP

DISH

SHOCK

SHACK

CASH

SHED

1. Practice as a class. 2. Practice individually. 3. Sign or stamp only when the student can read it on their own without help.

They dash to the shed. They find cash. What a shock!

Sign or Stamp

Students can work on this while you test them one on one on the previous page.

Review Assessments

A. Speaking

1. Practice as a class and in partners beforehand.
2. How many sentences can you make in a minute?

1. (question)   3. (question)   5. (question)   7. (question)
2. (answer)   4. (answer)   6. (answer)   8. (answer)

9. (question)   11. (question)   13. (question)   15. (question)
10. (answer)   12. (answer)   14. (answer)   16. (answer)

17. (question)   19. (question)   21. (question)   23. (question)
18. (answer)   20. (answer)   22. (answer)   24. (answer)

51

Review Assessments

B. Reading

How many letters and sounds can the student do in a minute without help?

He is a bad kid. He wants to kick a duck,	11
but a big duck kicks the kid. The kid is	21
mad. The kid wants to stick the duck in	30
a sack, but the duck is fast. The duck	39
runs back to the pond.	44

C. Listening

Ask each student individually without gestures of any kind. How many questions out of the total does the student respond correctly to?

1. How are you?
2. What is your name?
3. Go get a pencil and eraser, please.
4. Look at me, please.
5. Where is your textbook?
6. Turn to page five.
7. Where is your pencil.
8. Sit properly, please.
9. Don't fight, please. What do you do?

D. Spelling

See how many words the students can spell correctly. The teacher says the words one by one and the students spell the words out.

desk	and	check	fish
gift	went	catch	shack
are	want	the	black
he	they	watch	sand

Unit 9

Speaking Practice
Practice until students can say the words individually without help.

My mom doesn't like _____.

1 beetles	2 spiders	3 cockroaches
4 worms	5 mosquitoes	6 flies

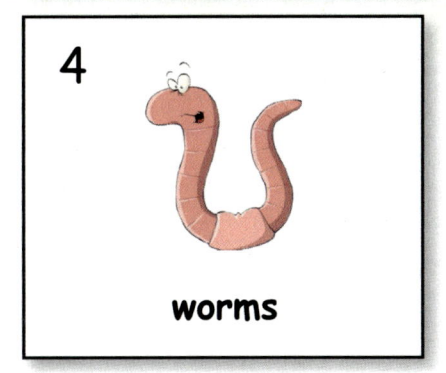

Listening Practice

Test each student individually. Ask the questions below without any gestures or help to see how well the student understands.

1. Hi, how are you?
2. What is your name?
3. What do you like to do?
4. What do you like to eat?
5. Does your mom like cockroaches?
6. Does your dad like mosquitoes?

Sign or Stamp

Reading Comprehension

Read, write and draw a line to the correct picture. Then color.

1. This is a hand.

   _____
   _____
   _____
   _____

2. This is a gift.

   _____
   _____
   _____
   _____

1. Practice as a class. 2. Practice individually. 3. Sign or stamp only when the student can read it on their own without help.

th

with
path
thin
this
that
than

Sight Word:
you

Spelling Words:

with
this
that
than

Sign or Stamp

Students can work on this while you test them one on one on the previous page.

Write and find.

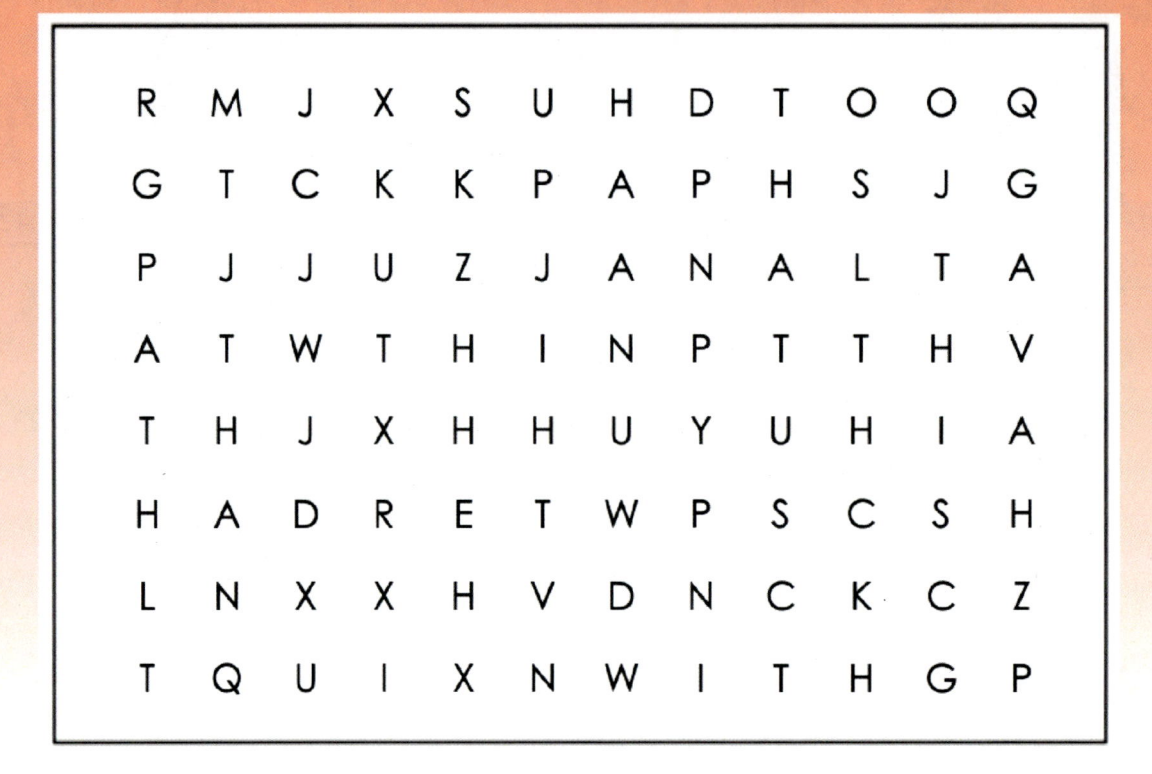

R	M	J	X	S	U	H	D	T	O	O	Q
G	T	C	K	K	P	A	P	H	S	J	G
P	J	J	U	Z	J	A	N	A	L	T	A
A	T	W	T	H	I	N	P	T	T	H	V
T	H	J	X	H	H	U	Y	U	H	I	A
H	A	D	R	E	T	W	P	S	C	S	H
L	N	X	X	H	V	D	N	C	K	C	Z
T	Q	U	I	X	N	W	I	T	H	G	P

WITH

THIS

PATH

THAT

THIN

THAN

56

1. Practice as a class. 2. Practice individually. 3. Sign or stamp only when the student can read it on their own without help.

You went on this path with a van. You went back. You went back into this pond.

Sign or Stamp

57

Students can work on this while you test them one on one on the previous page.

Unit 10

Speaking Practice
Practice until students can say the words individually without help.

My _____ doesn't like mosquitoes .

1 grandpa	2 grandma	3 big sister
4 little sister	5 big brother	6 little brother

Listening Practice

Test each student individually. Ask the questions below without any gestures or help to see how well the student understands.

1. Do you have any brothers or sisters?
2. How many brothers and sister do you have?
3. What are their names?
4. Do you have a grandma and grandpa?
5. Do they live in your house with you?
6. Does your dad like mosquitoes?

Sign or Stamp

Reading Comprehension

Read, write and draw a line to the correct picture. Then color.

1. You are Mom.

2. You are Dad.

60

1. Practice as a class. 2. Practice individually. 3. Sign or stamp only when the student can read it on their own without help.

l blends

clap
black
flick
slam
class
blast

Sight Word:

when
see

Spelling Words:

class
you
when
see

Sign or Stamp

61

Students can work on this while you test them one on one on the previous page.

Write and find.

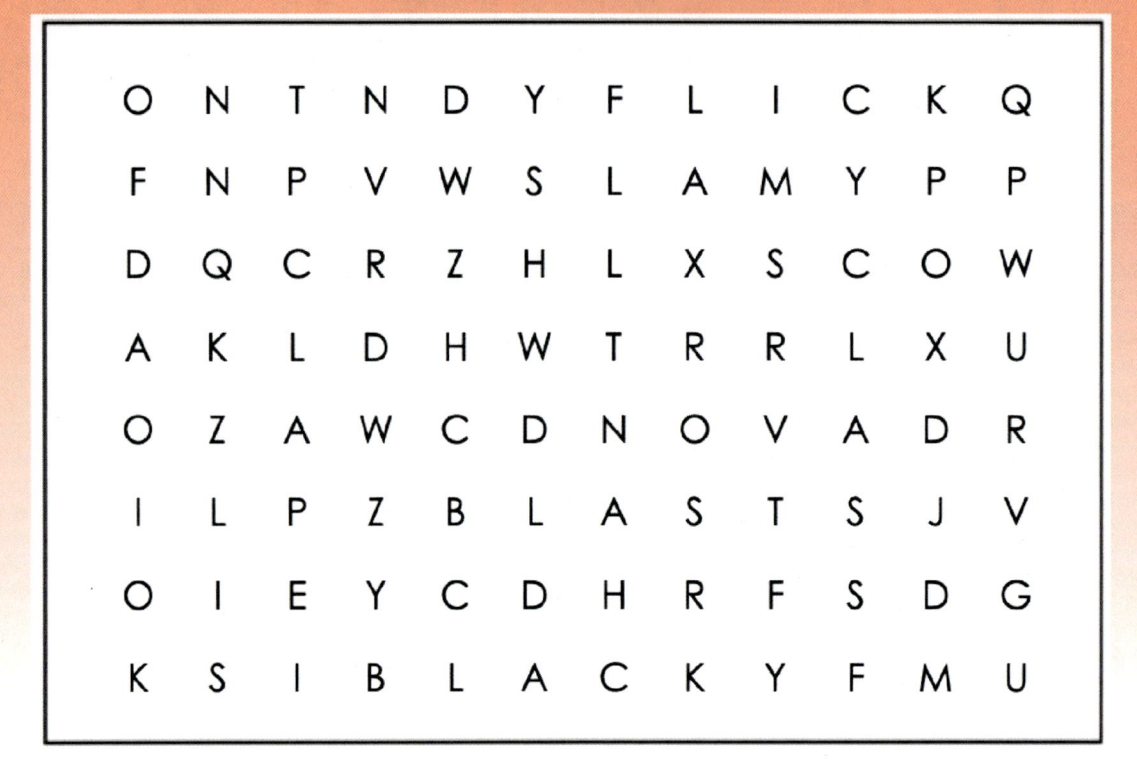

```
O N T N D Y F L I C K Q
F N P V W S L A M Y P P
D Q C R Z H L X S C O W
A K L D H W T R R L X U
O Z A W C D N O V A D R
I L P Z B L A S T S J V
O I E Y C D H R F S D G
K S I B L A C K Y F M U
```

CLAP   SLAM

BLACK   CLASS

FLICK   BLAST

62

1. Practice as a class. 2. Practice individually. 3. Sign or stamp only when the student can read it on their own without help.

The slug plans to go on the sled with the kid. When she sees the slug, she will be mad.

Sign or Stamp

Students can work on this while you test them one on one on the previous page.

Unit 11

Speaking Practice
Practice until students can say the words individually without help.

Can I borrow _____, please?

| 1 a pencil | 2 some glue | 3 some scissors |
| 4 some colored pencils | 5 a piece of paper | 6 a scary monster |

Speaking Practice

Practice as a class. Test each student individually. The student should be able to ask to borrow each thing in front of the teacher.

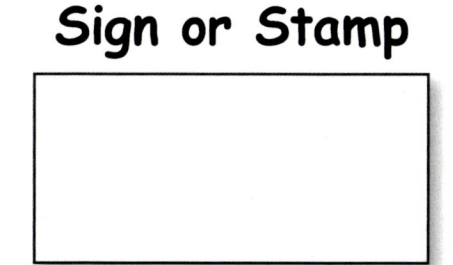

Sign or Stamp

65

Reading Comprehension

Read, write and draw a line to the correct picture. Then color.

1. The fish is in a truck.

2. The fish swims.

1. Practice as a class. 2. Practice individually. 3. Sign or stamp only when the student can read it on their own without help.

r blends

brick

crack

from

drip

truck

drift

Sight Words Review:

they

when

he

see

to

she

go

Spelling Words:

class

you

when

see

Sign or Stamp

Students can work on this while you test them one on one on the previous page.

Write and find.

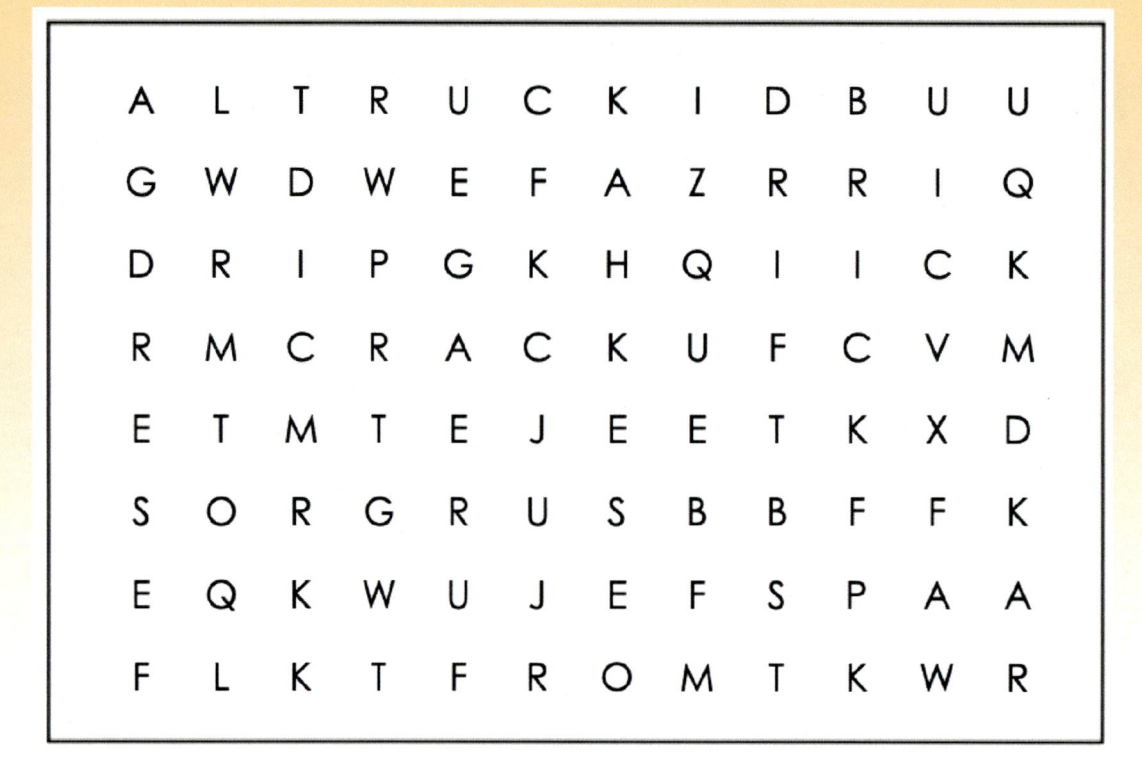

A	L	T	R	U	C	K	I	D	B	U	U
G	W	D	W	E	F	A	Z	R	R	I	Q
D	R	I	P	G	K	H	Q	I	I	C	K
R	M	C	R	A	C	K	U	F	C	V	M
E	T	M	T	E	J	E	E	T	K	X	D
S	O	R	G	R	U	S	B	B	F	F	K
E	Q	K	W	U	J	E	F	S	P	A	A
F	L	K	T	F	R	O	M	T	K	W	R

BRICK   DRIP

CRACK   TRUCK

FROM   DRIFT

68

1. Practice as a class. 2. Practice individually. 3. Sign or stamp only when the student can read it on their own without help.

They stop the truck. They pick up the trash. They put the trash in the truck.

Sign or Stamp

69

Students can work on this while you test them one on one on the previous page.

Unit 12

Speaking Practice

Practice until students can say the words individually without help.

What is there in the picture?
There is a _____.

1. tree
2. cloud
3. house
4. window
5. sky
6. sun

Speaking Practice

Practice as a class. Test each student individually. Students should be able to make good sentences about what there is in the picture.

Sign or Stamp

71

Reading Comprehension

Read, write and draw a line to the correct picture. Then color.

1. This pig sits on a red mat.
   _____
   _____
   _____

2. This pig stands on a black mat.
   _____
   _____
   _____

1. Practice as a class. 2. Practice individually. 3. Sign or stamp only when the student can read it on their own without help.

str
spr
scr
thr
shr

strip
sprint
scratch
thrash
shred

Spelling Words:
sprint
scratch
thrash
away

Sight Word:
away

Sign or Stamp

Students can work on this while you test them one on one on the previous page.

Write and find.

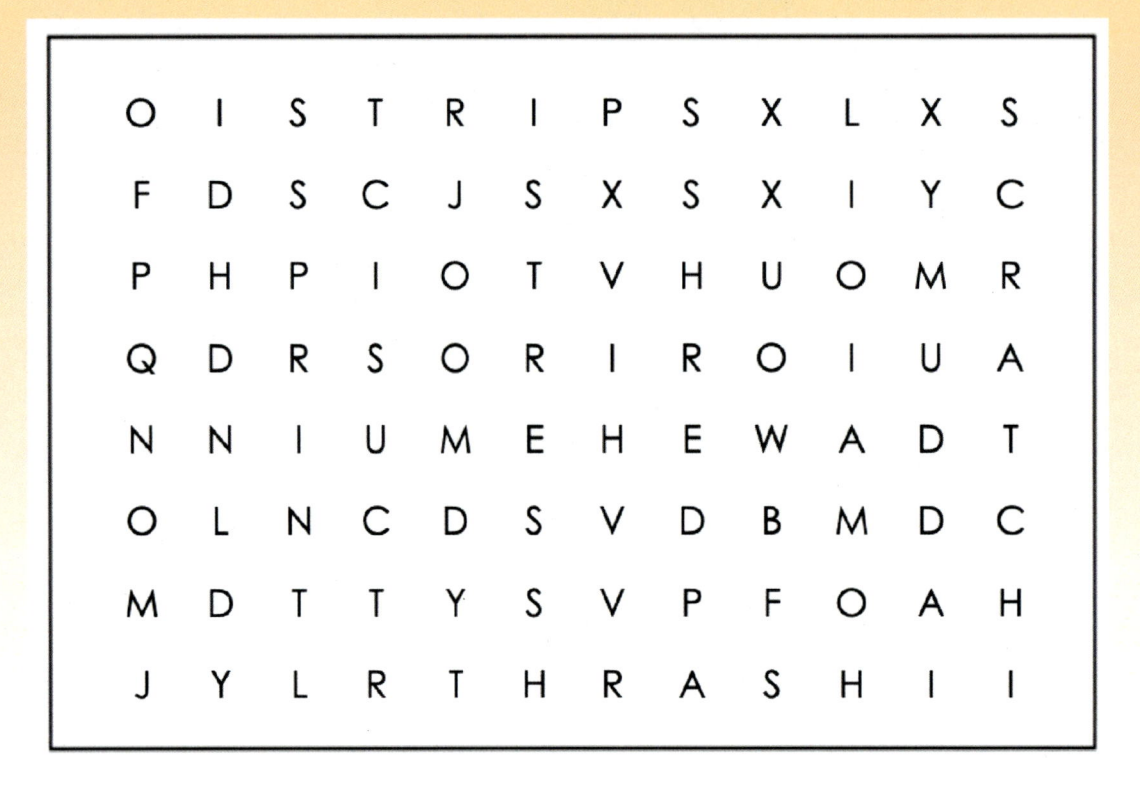

```
O  I  S  T  R  I  P  S  X  L  X  S
F  D  S  C  J  S  X  S  X  I  Y  C
P  H  P  I  O  T  V  H  U  O  M  R
Q  D  R  S  O  R  I  R  O  I  U  A
N  N  I  U  M  E  H  E  W  A  D  T
O  L  N  C  D  S  V  D  B  M  D  C
M  D  T  T  Y  S  V  P  F  O  A  H
J  Y  L  R  T  H  R  A  S  H  I  I
```

STRIP

THRASH

SPRINT

SHRED

SCRATCH

STRESS

74

1. Practice as a class. 2. Practice individually. 3. Sign or stamp only when the student can read it on their own without help.

The cat can scratch. It shreds the rug. It shreds the rug and sprints away.

Sign or Stamp

75

Students can work on this while you test them one on one on the previous page.

Review Assessments

A. Speaking

1. Practice as a class and in partners beforehand.
2. How many sentences can you make in a minute?

1.

2.

3.

4.

5.

6.

7.

8.

9.

10.

11.

12.

77

Review Assessments

B. Reading

How many letters and sounds can the student do in a minute without help?

The chick jumps and runs. The mom wants to catch	10
the chick, but the chick is fast. The chick runs into a	22
shack. The mom gets the chick and puts it in the soft	34
nest. The chick jumps and runs. It runs into a pond.	45
The chick jumps on a fish. The mom gets the chick and	57
puts it back in the nest. Bad chick!	65

C. Listening

Ask each student individually without gestures of any kind. How many questions out of the total does the student respond correctly to?

1. Do you have any brothers or sisters?
2. How many brothers and sister do you have?
3. What are their names?
4. Do you have a grandma and grandpa?
5. Does your dad like beetles?
6. Does your dad like mosquitoes?
7. Is there a sun in this picture?
8. How about a house?
9. What else is there in this picture?
10. Does your mom like cockroaches?

D. Spelling

See how many words the students can spell correctly. The teacher says the words one by one and the students spell the words out.

with	class	from	sprint
this	you	truck	scratch
that	when	he	thrash
than	see	go	away

Unit 13

Speaking Practice

Practice until students can say the words individually without help.

Which animal do you like most? I like the _____ the most.

1 bird	2 giraffe	3 lion
4 kangaroo	5 hippo	6 elephant

Speaking Practice

Practice as a class. Test each student individually. Students should be able to make good sentences about what there is in the picture and which they like best.

Sign or Stamp

79

Reading Comprehension

Read, write and draw a line to the correct picture. Then color.

1. The squid checks on the ship.

2. The kids on the ship see a squid.

80

1. Practice as a class. 2. Practice individually. 3. Sign or stamp only when the student can read it on their own without help.

qu

squ

quit

quack

quiz

quest

squid

squish

Sight Word:

away

Spelling Words:

quit
squid
squish
goes

Sign or Stamp

Students can work on this while you test them one on one on the previous page.

Write and find.

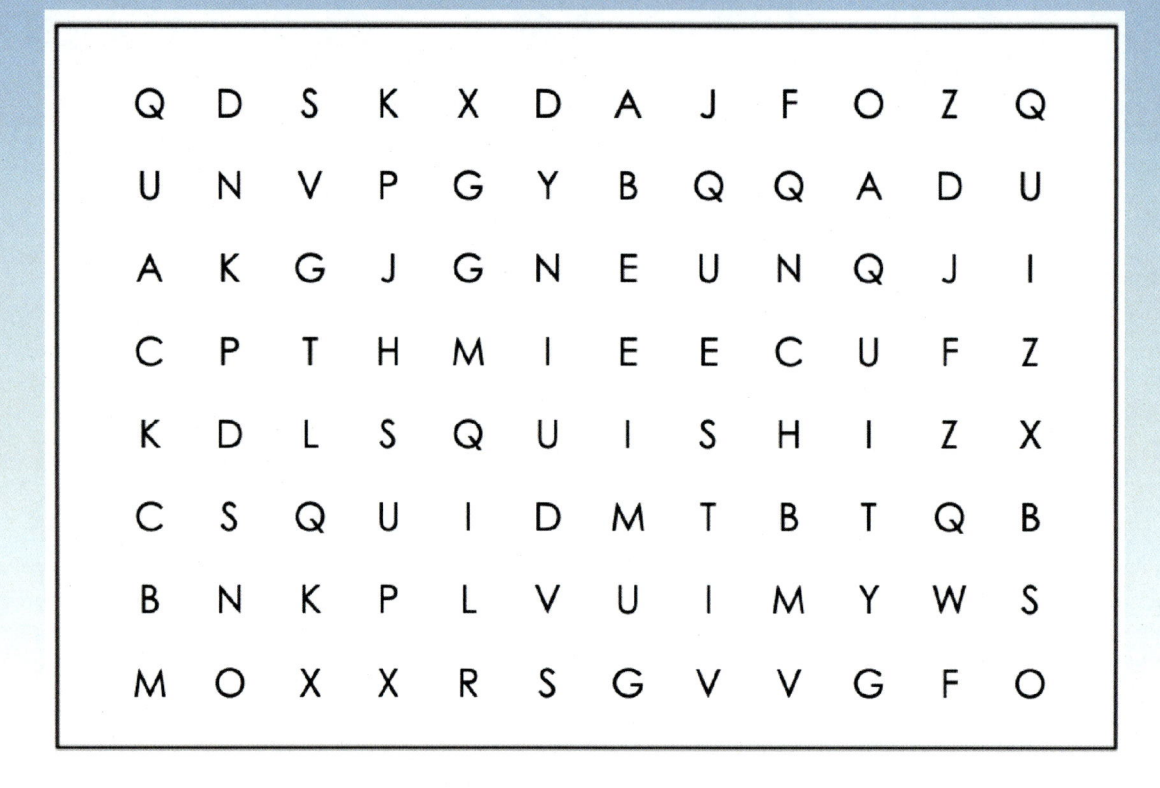

Q	D	S	K	X	D	A	J	F	O	Z	Q
U	N	V	P	G	Y	B	Q	Q	A	D	U
A	K	G	J	G	N	E	U	N	Q	J	I
C	P	T	H	M	I	E	E	C	U	F	Z
K	D	L	S	Q	U	I	S	H	I	Z	X
C	S	Q	U	I	D	M	T	B	T	Q	B
B	N	K	P	L	V	U	I	M	Y	W	S
M	O	X	X	R	S	G	V	V	G	F	O

QUIT   QUEST

QUACK   SQUID

QUIZ   SQUISH

82

1. Practice as a class. 2. Practice individually. 3. Sign or stamp only when the student can read it on their own without help.

Jack goes on a quest. He steps in some muck. Squish. Yuck! He finds some bats. Ah! Run away! Jacks quits the quest.

Sign or Stamp

Students can work on this while you test them one on one on the previous page.

Unit 14

Speaking Practice
Practice until students can say the words individually without help.

How is the weather today?
It is _____.

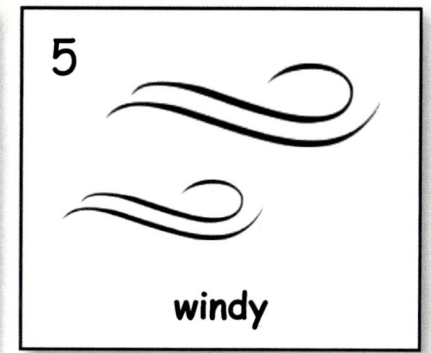

1 snowy	2 rainy	3 sunny
4 cloudy	5 windy	6 stormy

Weather Game

Play the weather game. The teacher calls out the type of weather and everyone acts out what you do in that weather. The last person to do it is out.

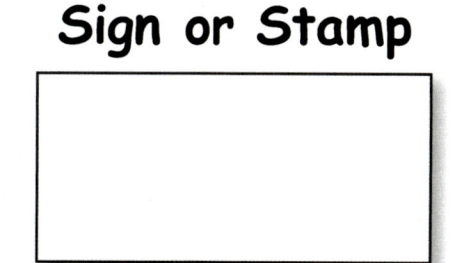

Sign or Stamp

Reading Comprehension

Read, write and draw a line to the correct picture. Then color.

1. The strong kid can lift.

2. The quick kid can run.

1. Practice as a class. 2. Practice individually. 3. Sign or stamp only when the student can read it on their own without help.

ing
ng
nk

ring
string
strong
sink
skunk
think

Spelling Words:
sing
long
strong
think

Sight Word:
too
one

Sign or Stamp

87

Students can work on this while you test them one on one on the previous page.

Write and find.

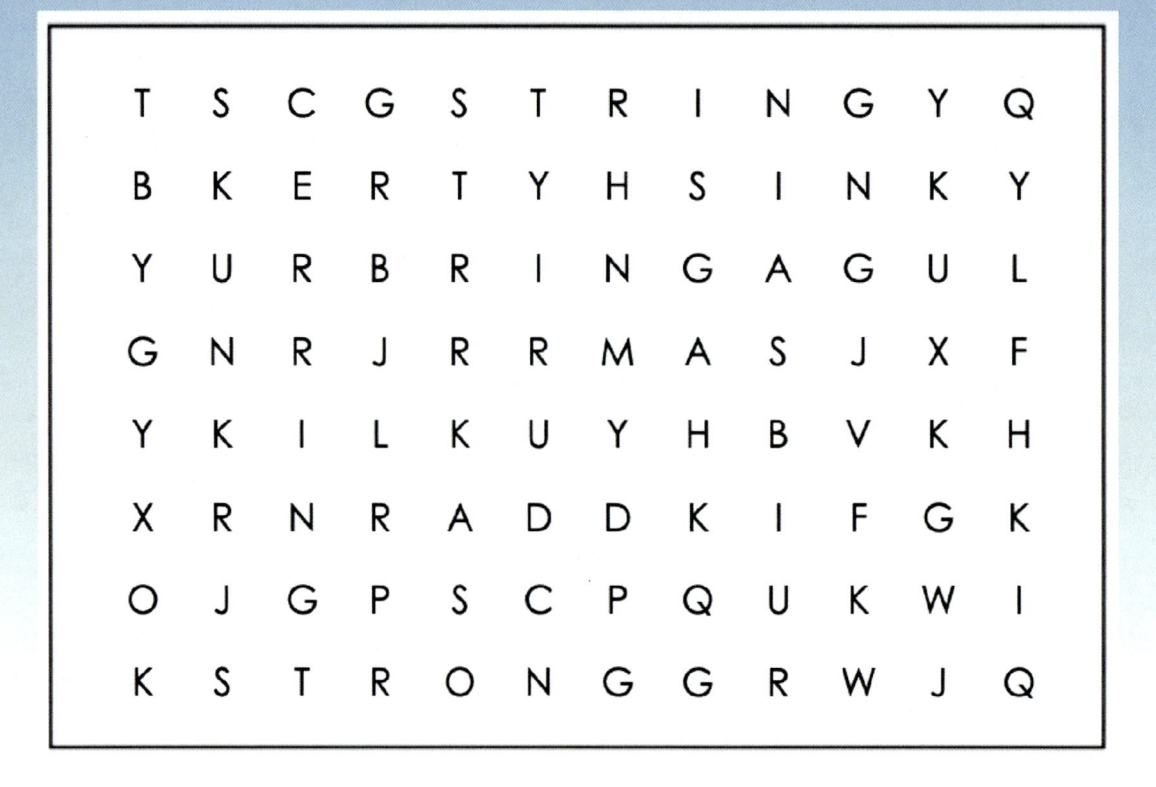

T	S	C	G	S	T	R	I	N	G	Y	Q
B	K	E	R	T	Y	H	S	I	N	K	Y
Y	U	R	B	R	I	N	G	A	G	U	L
G	N	R	J	R	R	M	A	S	J	X	F
Y	K	I	L	K	U	Y	H	B	V	K	H
X	R	N	R	A	D	D	K	I	F	G	K
O	J	G	P	S	C	P	Q	U	K	W	I
K	S	T	R	O	N	G	G	R	W	J	Q

RING

BRING

STRING

SKUNK

STRONG

SINK

1. Practice as a class. 2. Practice individually. 3. Sign or stamp only when the student can read it on their own without help.

The skunks go on the path. The skunks stink. One skunks brings a mask. It thinks the skunks stink too much! Yuck!

Sign or Stamp

Students can work on this while you test them one on one on the previous page.

Unit 15

Speaking Practice

Practice until students can say the words individually without help.

What do you need to wear?
I need to wear _____.

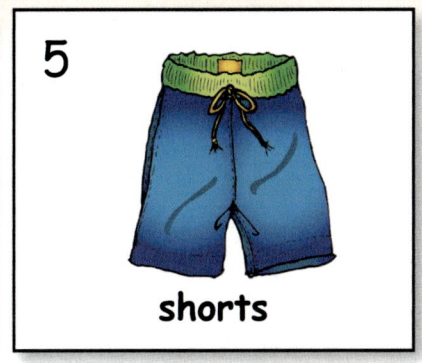

1 a coat	2 a jacket	3 a T-shirt
4 a sweater	5 shorts	6 pants

Listening Practice

Test each student individually. Ask the questions below without any gestures or help to see how well the student understands.

1. It's snowy and cold outside. What do you need to wear?
2. It's sunny and hot outside. What do you need to wear?
3. How many people are in your family?
4. Who are they?

Sign or Stamp

91

Reading Comprehension

Read, write and draw a line to the correct picture. Then color.

1. She has a strong kick.

2. The rabbit sings a song.

1. Practice as a class. 2. Practice individually. 3. Sign or stamp only when the student can read it on their own without help.

ll
le

well

spell

little

puzzle

simple

uncle

Sight Words Review:

are
want
watch
find
what
too
away
one

Spelling Words:

well
tell
little
one

Sign or Stamp

Students can work on this while you test them one on one on the previous page.

Write and find.

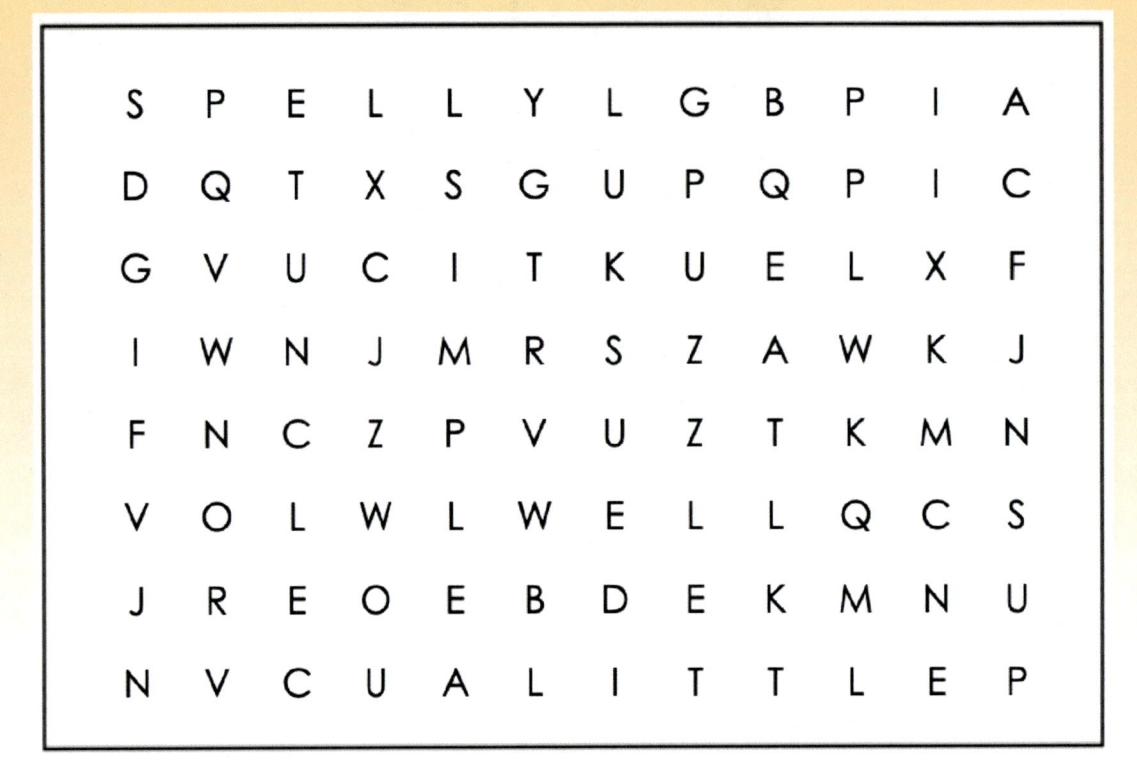

S	P	E	L	L	Y	L	G	B	P	I	A
D	Q	T	X	S	G	U	P	Q	P	I	C
G	V	U	C	I	T	K	U	E	L	X	F
I	W	N	J	M	R	S	Z	A	W	K	J
F	N	C	Z	P	V	U	Z	T	K	M	N
V	O	L	W	L	W	E	L	L	Q	C	S
J	R	E	O	E	B	D	E	K	M	N	U
N	V	C	U	A	L	I	T	T	L	E	P

WELL

PUZZLE

SPELL

SIMPLE

LITTLE

UNCLE

94

1. Practice as a class. 2. Practice individually. 3. Sign or stamp only when the student can read it on their own without help.

She brings a dog to class. The man sees the dog. He is mad. Then the bell rings. Quick! Get going!

Sign or Stamp

Students can work on this while you test them one on one on the previous page.

Review Assessments

A. Speaking

1. Practice as a class and in partners beforehand.
2. How many sentences can you make in a minute?

1. (question)   3. (question)   5. (question)   7. (question)
2. (answer)   4. (answer)   6. (answer)   8. (answer)

9. (question)   11. (question) 13. (question) 15. (question)
10. (answer)   12. (answer)   14. (answer)   16. (answer)

17. (question) 19. (question) 21. (question) 23. (question)
18. (answer)   20. (answer)   22. (answer)   24. (answer)

97

Review Assessments

B. Reading

How many letters and sounds can the student do in a minute without help?

The crab gets up to sing. The crab slips. He hits his shins. Ug! The crab is sad. He sits. He wants to quit. A mom crab sees the sad crab. You can do it! The crab gets up. The crab wants to sing. The crab sings strong. He has a blast. His song rings. The crabs and fish clap. The crabs and fish bring him gifts. Then, he sees the mom crab. Thank you!	12 24 36 47 58 69 75

C. Listening

Ask each student individually without gestures of any kind. How many questions out of the total does the student respond correctly to?

1. Which animal do you like most?
2. Do you like lions?
3. How about kangaroos?
4. How is the weather today?
5. Is it stormy outside?
6. If it is stormy and cold outside, what do you need to wear?
7. If it is sunny and hot outside, what do you need to wear?
8. Do you like to read?

D. Spelling

See how many words the students can spell correctly. The teacher says the words one by one and the students spell the words out.

quit	sing	well	they
squid	long	tell	you
squish	strong	little	she
goes	think	one	are

Copyright 2021

Kid-Inspired Classroom

All rights reserved. No part of this book may be reproduced in any form.

Made in the USA
Las Vegas, NV
16 April 2024